SCORPIO:

A COMPLETE GUIDE TO THE SCORPIO ASTROLOGY STAR SIGN

Sofia Visconti

Contents

INTRODUCTION 1
Compatibility 2
Personality Traits 3
Strengths 4
Weaknesses 4

CHAPTER 1: HISTORY AND MYTHOLOGY 6
Babylon 6
Ancient Egypt 7
Ancient Greek 7
Chinese 8
Indian 8
Mayan 8
Historical Events Under the Scorpio Sign 9
Historical Figures Born Under Scorpio 10
Further Reading and References 11

CHAPTER 2: LOVE & COMPATIBILITY 13
Scorpio and Aries 16
Scorpio and Taurus 16
Scorpio and Gemini 17
Scorpio and Cancer 17
Scorpio and Leo 17
Scorpio and Virgo 17
Scorpio and Libra 18
Scorpio and Scorpio 18
Scorpio and Sagittarius 18
Scorpio and Capricorn 18
Scorpio and Aquarius 19
Scorpio and Pisces 19

Tips for Men Dating Scorpio Women 20
Tips for Women Dating Scorpio Men 21

CHAPTER 3: FRIENDS AND FAMILY............................. 24

CHAPTER 4: CAREER AND MONEY................................ 33
Intensity and Emotional Expression 39
Tendency to Hold Grudges... 40
Desire for Control 40
Resistance to Change.. 40
Tendency Toward Secrecy... 41
Difficulty in Accepting Constructive Criticism........................... 41
Overwhelm from High Expectations 41

CHAPTER 5: SELF-IMPROVEMENT 44
Utilizing Strengths.. 47
Overcoming Weaknesses... 48
Seeking Support 50

CHAPTER 6: THE YEAR AHEAD 52
Love and Relationships... 54
Solar and Lunar Eclipses 58
Mercury Retrograde 59
Jupiter Transits 59
Saturn Transits.. 59
Venus Retrograde 60
Mars Transits 60
New Moon and Full Moon Phases 60

CHAPTER 7: FAMOUS SCORPIO PERSONALITIES...... 63

CONCLUSION 73

INTRODUCTION

Throughout history humans have yearned to find significance and direction through the bodies that grace our night sky. This timeless practice, known as astrology, weaves together elements of science, symbolism and spirituality. At its core, astrology is a belief system centered around the idea that the positions and movements of objects like stars and planets can influence our lives here on Earth. It rests upon the belief that the alignment of these bodies at the moment of an individual's birth can provide insights into their personality traits, destiny and life experiences. Various systems and traditions fall under astrologys umbrella. Western astrology stands as its most widely recognized form. This system revolves around twelve zodiac signs, each linked to characteristics and personality traits.

In this book we embark on a journey to explore one of the signs, in the zodiac. Scorpio. Represented by the scorpion, it is known for its intense emotions, passion and transformative nature. In this book's pages we will explore the essence of Scorpio in depth. We'll delve into its symbolism, personality traits, strengths, weaknesses and compatibility with other signs. Our goal is to unravel the mysteries surrounding Scorpio and reveal its hidden aspects. In turn you can gain an understanding of either yourself or the Scorpios in your life.

OVERVIEW OF SCORPIO ZODIAC SIGN

- **Date of Star Sign**: October 23 - November 21.
- **Symbol**: Scorpion. The scorpion symbolizes the sign's intensity, determination and capability for transformation.
- **Element**: Water. Scorpio is associated with the water element. This element signifies Scorpio's emotional depth and sensitivity.
- **Planet**: Pluto (Traditional ruler: Mars). Pluto symbolizes transformation, power and rebirth. Mars, the ancient ruler, adds an element of action, assertiveness and energy.
- **Color**: Deep and intense shades such as dark red, maroon and black. These colors reflect Scorpio's passion, mystery and depth.

COMPATIBILITY

Scorpios compatibility can vary depending on the zodiac sign of the person. Scorpios tend to build strong connections, with signs like Cancer, Pisces and other

Scorpios because they share emotional depth and intuition. They may have passionate relationships with Taurus and Leo. However it's important to remember that compatibility also relies on personalities and how well they complement each other's strengths and weaknesses.

PERSONALITY TRAITS

Scorpio individuals are known for their intense and complex personalities. Here are some key personality traits associated with Scorpio.

- **Passionate**: Scorpios are incredibly passionate and driven. They approach life with intensity and commitment. Energy is poured into their pursuits and relationships.
- **Determined**: Scorpios are highly determined and persistent. Once they set their sights on a goal, they will stop at nothing to achieve it. Their strong willpower often leads them to success.
- **Mysterious**: Scorpios have a mysterious aura about them. They tend to keep their true feelings and thoughts guarded. Only revealing what they choose to share. This enigmatic quality adds to their allure.
- **Resilient**: Scorpios possess remarkable resilience. They have the ability to bounce back from adversity and transform challenges into opportunities.
- **Resourceful**: Scorpios are resourceful problem solvers. They have a knack for finding creative solutions to complex problems. As such they are not easily deterred by obstacles.

STRENGTHS

- **Loyal**: Scorpios are fiercely loyal to their friends and loved ones. They will stand by your side through thick and thin.
- **Brave**: They have a fearless nature and are unafraid to confront difficult situations or truths.
- **Determined**: Scorpios have an unwavering determination to succeed in their endeavors.
- **Intuitive**: Their strong intuition allows them to read people and situations well, making them excellent judges of character.
- **Passionate**: Scorpios bring an intense passion to everything they do. This makes them magnetic and captivating individuals.

WEAKNESSES

- **Jealous**: Scorpios can be prone to jealousy and possessiveness. This sometimes leads to conflicts.
- **Secretive**: They tend to keep their emotions and thoughts hidden. Overall this can make things challenging for others to truly understand them.
- **Stubborn**: Scorpios can be incredibly stubborn. Once they make up their minds, it's challenging to change their course.
- **Vindictive**: When wronged, Scorpios can hold grudges and seek revenge.
- **Intense**: Their intensity can be overwhelming for some. Clashes may occur in personal and professional relationships.

As we journey through the pages of this book you can anticipate discovering the many aspects of Scorpios energy, strengths and weaknesses. Furthermore we will provide insights to help you navigate relationships with Scorpios or gain a deeper understanding of yourself if you were born under this sign. This exploration will take us on a voyage as we unlock the mysteries of Scorpio. One that will tap into its power for personal growth, meaningful connections with others and a greater appreciation for how the universe subtly influences our lives. So go ahead and turn the page. It's time to embark on this captivating journey into the enigmatic realm of Scorpio.

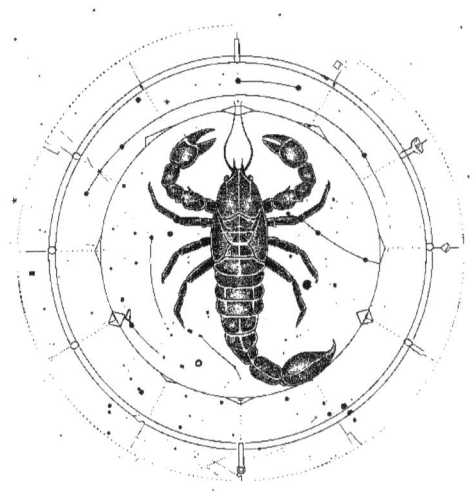

CHAPTER 1: HISTORY AND MYTHOLOGY

The Scorpio constellation, a prominent and distinctive figure in the night sky, has captured the imagination of humans for millennia. Its historical and mythological origins vary across different ancient civilizations. Each offers unique insights into how Scorpio was observed and represented in their star maps. Let's take a closer look.

EARLIEST OBSERVATIONS IN ANCIENT CIVILIZATIONS

BABYLON

The origins of Scorpio can be traced back to ancient Babylon, where it was known as "MUL.GIR.TAB," meaning "the scorpion." The Babylonians were meticulous astronomers who associated this constellation with the goddess Ishtar. They believed Scorpio's appearance in the sky was significant for predicting weather patterns and agricultural cycles.

ANCIENT EGYPT

In ancient Egypt, Scorpio held great significance. The constellation was closely linked to the goddess Serqet, often depicted with a scorpion's head. Serqet was a protective deity associated with medicine and healing. Scorpio's appearance in the night sky was considered a symbol of transformation, renewal and protection.

ANCIENT GREEK

In Greek mythology, Scorpio is associated with the story of Orion. A giant scorpion sent by Gaia to defeat him. This battle resulted in Orion's demise and the scorpion was placed in the heavens as a constellation. Scorpio symbolizes the consequences of hubris and revenge.

CHINESE

In Chinese astronomy, Scorpio is not an independent constellation but is part of the Azure Dragon of the East. It represents autumn and the metal element. This plays a key role in Chinese astrology and cosmology.

INDIAN

In Hindu astrology, Scorpio corresponds to the nakshatra (lunar mansion) called Anuradha. Anuradha represents success through determination, devotion and friendship. It is associated with the Hindu god Mitra. She is a deity of contracts and friendship.

MAYAN

The ancient Maya had their own interpretations of celestial objects, including Scorpio. They likely incorporated into their complex calendar systems and mythologies.

The above are all diverse cultural perceptions and representations of Scorpio. All highlight the multifaceted nature of human understanding of the night sky. Scorpio's enduring presence in mythology and astronomy serves as a testament to humanity's timeless fascination with the cosmos.

Throughout ancient civilizations, Scorpio held an important place. As time progressed astrology transformed to introspective and personality focused perspectives. Nowadays Scorpio is associated with depth, passion and personal transformation. Those born under this sign are believed to possess qualities such as intensity, resourcefulness and a sincere desire for authenticity.

HISTORICAL EVENTS UNDER THE SCORPIO SIGN

The Scorpio season has witnessed significant historical events. While it's important to note that astrology doesn't provide explanations for these events, some intriguing occurrences have taken place during this period.

- **The Russian Revolution (October 1917)**: This pivotal event in world history, began in October 1917. Scorpio's association with transformation and upheaval aligns with the radical changes that occurred during this time. Ultimately it led to the establishment of the Soviet Union.
- **The Cuban Missile Crisis (October 1962)**: Scorpio's intensity and potential for power struggles were evident during this tense confrontation between the United States and the Soviet Union. It almost brought the world to the brink of nuclear war.
- **The Fall of the Berlin Wall (November 1989)**: Scorpio's theme of rebirth and transformation resonates with the fall of the Berlin Wall. This event symbolized the end of the Cold War era and the reunification of Germany.

HISTORICAL FIGURES BORN UNDER SCORPIO

Several influential historical figures were born under the Scorpio sign. They showcase the diversity of impact and personality traits associated with this sign.

- **Marie Curie (November 7, 1867):** The pioneering physicist and chemist who conducted groundbreaking research on radioactivity. Her relentless determination and transformative discoveries align with Scorpio traits.
- **Martin Luther (November 10, 1483):** The leader of the Protestant Reformation who challenged

established norms and ignited religious and social change. His personality resonates with Scorpio's propensity for transformation.
- **Indira Gandhi (November 19, 1917)**: India's first female Prime Minister who exhibited Scorpio's determination, leadership, and intense commitment to her political ideals.

As we conclude this chapter with contemplation we acknowledge the tapestry of stories and historical significance surrounding the constellation of Scorpio. From its early observations by ancient civilizations to its diverse mythological interpretations over time. Scorpio has consistently captivated human imagination. Its influence transcends time leaving a lasting impact, on both the past and present. In today's astrology Scorpio holds a key position. One for providing understanding into the intricate aspects of human behavior. Whether delving into one's mind or deciphering the complexities of relationships. Scorpio remains meaningful and relatable in our lives.

FURTHER READING AND REFERENCES

For those who wish to delve deeper into the history and mythology of Scorpio, here is a list of primary sources, ancient texts and modern writings.

Primary Sources and Ancient Texts:

- "Enuma Anu Enlil" - An ancient Babylonian cuneiform text that contains references to Scorpio and its astrological significance.

- "Book of the Dead" - Egyptian funerary texts that mention the protective deity Serqet, associated with the Scorpio constellation.
- Classical Greek and Roman mythology texts, including the works of Hesiod, Ovid, and Homer, which feature stories related to Scorpio.

Modern Writings

- "The Only Astrology Book You'll Ever Need" by Joanna Martine Woolfolk - A comprehensive guide to astrology that includes insights into Scorpio and its characteristics.
- "The Secret Language of Birthdays" by Gary Goldschneider and Joost Elffers - This book explores the personality traits associated with each day of the year, offering insights into Scorpio birthdays.
- "Astrology: The Twelve Zodiac Signs" by Judy Hall - A book that provides a detailed overview of each zodiac sign, including Scorpio, with a focus on personality traits and compatibility.
- "The Inner Sky: How to Make Wiser Choices for a More Fulfilling Life" by Steven Forrest - This book delves into the psychological and spiritual dimensions of astrology, including Scorpio's transformative potential.

CHAPTER 2:
LOVE & COMPATIBILITY

In this chapter we embark on a journey into the world of love and relationships focusing on the perspective of individuals born under the Scorpio zodiac sign. Scorpios are known for their aura and deep emotional nature, which provides a viewpoint on romantic connections. This chapter will guide you in understanding the intricacies and subtleties of Scorpios language of love. From their needs to their unwavering loyalty we will dissect what makes love such an all encompassing experience for Scorpios.

We will also delve into the dynamics of communication and trust within Scorpio relationships illuminating how these crucial aspects foster connections for them. Additionally we'll explore the compatibility between Scorpios and other zodiac signs shedding light on both the synergies and challenges that may arise in these unions.

Lastly this chapter aims to dispel misconceptions about Scorpios in matters of love by providing an understanding of their true romantic nature. Throughout this journey you will acquire understanding of the realm of love and relationships as experienced by Scorpio individuals. Brace yourself to explore the depths of Scorpio, where intensity and passion intertwine with vulnerability and profoundness.

LOVE APPROACH

Scorpio is often associated with a sense of intensity, passion and a strong desire for connection. Individuals born under this water sign, tend to approach matters of the heart with a blend of intrigue and fervor. Let's take a closer look at how Scorpios approach love and romance.

- **Intense Passion**; Scorpios are renowned for their intense nature. When they fall in love they do so with their whole being. They crave deep connections and are willing to invest into nurturing their relationships. This intensity can create a whirlwind of emotions in their love lives which can be both exhilarating and challenging.
- **Emotional Depth**; Scorpios have mastered the art of delving into the depths of their emotions.

They fearlessly confront not only their feelings but also those of their partners. This emotional honesty often leads to close intimacy and strong bonds.
- **Loyalty**; Once committed to a relationship Scorpios display unwavering loyalty. As such they expect the level of commitment from their partners. Meanwhile they occasionally exhibit possessiveness.
- **Unforgiving**; Scorpios are known for their unforgiving nature, driven by their need to safeguard what they hold dear. Betrayal can have a negative impact on them making it difficult for them to forgive and forget.
- **Mysterious**; Scorpios tend to have a mysterious aura. They tend to keep some secrets and emotions hidden. This can be both captivating and alluring to partners. Mystery adds excitement to relationships keeping their partners guessing and intrigued.
- **Overprotective**; Scorpios should be aware that they can sometimes experience feelings of jealousy and possessiveness. As such they may find themselves becoming overly protective of their partners or struggling with trust issues. It is important for them to strike a balance in order to maintain a relationship.
- **Controlling**; Scorpios are naturally drawn towards power and control in their relationships. Typically they seek partners who complement this desire. However it is crucial for them to manage this need for control carefully. Sometimes it can lead to power struggles within the relationship.

- **Sensuality**; Scorpios take pleasure in exploring their sensuality. They are often regarded as sexual individuals who deeply appreciate physical intimacy.
- **Transformative**; When it comes to love Scorpios have a passionate and all encompassing approach. They are known for their ability to bring about transformation and healing in their partners through profound experiences.

In summary Scorpios approach love with passion, emotional depth, loyalty and an air of mystery. While they possess a charm they also face challenges, like jealousy and possessiveness. Overall this requires collaboration and navigation in their relationships.

SCORPIO LOVE AND COMPATIBILITY WITH OTHER ZODIAC SIGNS

SCORPIO AND ARIES

Scorpio and Aries share a powerful and passionate connection. Both signs are intense and strong-willed. They are drawn to each other's energy and love challenges. This can lead to fiery clashes or incredible chemistry. Communication and compromise are essential for this relationship to thrive.

SCORPIO AND TAURUS

Scorpio and Taurus are opposites in the zodiac. This can create a magnetic attraction. Scorpio's intensity may initially intrigue Taurus. However their stubbornness can lead to conflicts. Shared desire for loyalty and commitment can make this relationship work with effort and patience.

SCORPIO AND GEMINI

Scorpio and Gemini have different approaches to life and love. Scorpio values depth and emotional connection. Gemini seeks variety and mental stimulation. These differences can create misunderstandings. Although with open communication and compromise, they can learn from each other and grow.

SCORPIO AND CANCER

Scorpio and Cancer are a natural match in the zodiac. Both signs prioritize emotional connection and nurturing. Their shared empathy and intuition create a strong bond. They easily understand each other's needs. This relationship is often characterized by deep intimacy and loyalty.

SCORPIO AND LEO

Scorpio and Leo are both strong-willed signs, which can lead to power struggles. However, their intense personalities can also fuel a passionate connection. With respect for each other's need for recognition and control, they can build a dynamic and exciting relationship.

SCORPIO AND VIRGO

Scorpio and Virgo share a deep appreciation for detail and a desire for perfection. While they have different ways of expressing it, their mutual dedication and work ethic can create a harmonious partnership. Overall they can complement each other well if they focus on their strengths.

SCORPIO AND LIBRA

Scorpio and Libra have contrasting approaches to relationships. Scorpio seeks depth and intensity. Libra values balance and harmony. This can lead to conflicts. However if they can find common ground and compromise, their differences can create a well-rounded partnership.

SCORPIO AND SCORPIO

Two Scorpios together can be a passionate and intense combination. They understand each other's emotional depth and need for loyalty. However, their possessiveness and jealousy can lead to power struggles. Trust is key for this relationship to work.

SCORPIO AND SAGITTARIUS

Scorpio and Sagittarius have different outlooks on life and love. Scorpio seeks depth and commitment. Sagittarius values freedom and adventure. These differences can create challenges. Although if they can find a balance, they can make it work.

SCORPIO AND CAPRICORN

Scorpio and Capricorn share a practical and goal-oriented approach to life. They both value commitment and loyalty. This can create a stable and enduring partnership. Their shared determination can help them overcome obstacles together.

SCORPIO AND AQUARIUS

Scorpio and Aquarius have very different personalities and values. Scorpio values emotional depth. Aquarius is more detached and intellectual. Building trust and understanding can be a challenge. However, if they can appreciate each other's uniqueness, they can find common ground.

SCORPIO AND PISCES

Scorpio and Pisces are both water signs, making for a deep and emotionally intuitive connection. They share a profound understanding of each other's feelings and desires. This relationship is often marked by empathy, creativity and a strong spiritual connection.

In astrology, while compatibility can be influenced by sun signs, it's essential to consider the entire birth chart for a more accurate assessment of a relationship's dynamics. Many other factors, such as moon signs, rising signs, and planetary placements, play a significant role in compatibility.

DATING AND RELATIONSHIPS

When it comes to dating and relationships with Scorpio individuals it can be thrilling and intense. Scorpios are famous for their passionate, loyal and intense disposition. Whether you're a man or woman looking to date or maintain a relationship with a Scorpio partner, here are some pointers to guide you.

TIPS FOR MEN DATING SCORPIO WOMEN

- **Honesty**: Scorpio women value honesty and authenticity above all else. Don't try to hide your feelings or intentions. They can easily detect deception. Be open about your emotions and thoughts.
- **Show Loyalty:** Loyalty is a crucial aspect of any relationship with a Scorpio woman. Once she commits to you, she expects the same level of commitment in return. Flirting with others or showing signs of disloyalty can lead to trust issues.
- **Respect Her Independence**: Scorpio women are strong and independent individuals. Respect her need for personal space. Don't try to control or possess her. Encourage her to pursue her passions and interests.
- Embrace Her Intensity: Scorpio women are known for their intense emotions. Be prepared to handle their deep feelings. Don't shy away from discussing emotional topics. Show empathy and understanding when she's going through challenging times.
- **Surprise Her**: Scorpio women appreciate thoughtfulness and surprises. Plan special and meaningful gestures to keep the relationship exciting and show your commitment.
- **Communicate Openly**: Effective communication is essential in any relationship. Particularly with Scorpio women. They value deep

conversations. They want to know your thoughts and feelings. Avoid being evasive or non-committal.

TIPS FOR WOMEN DATING SCORPIO MEN

- **Respect His Privacy**: Scorpio men can be quite secretive. They value their privacy. Avoid prying too much into their personal affairs. Allow them space to open up at their own pace.
- **Show Trust**: Trust is vital for Scorpio men. If you want to maintain a relationship with them. Trust them and do not engage in unnecessary jealousy or possessiveness.
- **Be Independent**: Scorpio men are attracted to strong, independent women. Women who have their own goals and passions. Maintain your individuality and encourage him to do the same.

- **Enjoy Intimacy:** Scorpio men are known for their passion and sensuality. Embrace this aspect of your relationship and explore your physical connection together.
- **Handle Conflicts Maturely**: Scorpio men can be intense and argumentative. Maintain your composure. Try to resolve issues through calm and rational discussions. Avoid escalating arguments.
- **Share Your Thoughts**: Scorpio men appreciate partners who can engage in deep and meaningful conversations. Share your thoughts, ideas and feelings openly. This will help you connect on a more profound level.

Regardless of whether you're a man or a woman it's important to keep in mind that every Scorpio individual is unique. As such their compatibility and preferences may differ. Ultimately a relationship with a Scorpio requires patience, understanding and an openness to embrace their passionate nature. By respecting their boundaries, being honest and nurturing the connection you can create a fulfilling and long lasting partnership with a Scorpio.

As we wrap up this chapter one thing is abundantly clear. Scorpio individuals aren't just searching for love. They yearn for connections that touch the depths of their soul. They're willing to put their heart and soul into love. For them it's a profound experience that requires openness, trust and a willingness to delve into the depths of the human heart. While there might be challenges arising from their possessiveness or occasional bouts of jealousy. Scorpios have the ability to bring about healing and personal growth in their partners.

As we continue our exploration of Scorpio's personality we invite you to carry these insights with you. Whether you are a Scorpio seeking love or someone lucky to have encountered the magnetic allure of this zodiac sign. May you embrace the intensity, value the depth and relish in the power that Scorpio love brings into your life.

CHAPTER 3:
FRIENDS AND FAMILY

In this chapter we are about to embark on a journey into the world of Scorpio individuals and their relationships with friends and family. Scorpios have a reputation for being intense, passionate and complex. These unique qualities shape the dynamics within their friendships and families. By reading this chapter you'll gain insight into the intricacies as strengths and challenges of being in a Scorpios inner circle. Whether you're a Scorpio seeking understanding of your place in friendship or family dynamics. Or simply curious about how Scorpios approach these relationships from others. Together let's uncover the depths of Scorpios relationships and witness the transformative power they hold.

FRIENDSHIPS

Having a friend who's a Scorpio is like having a devoted companion who will support you unconditionally. Scorpios possess qualities that make them fascinating and dependable as friends. Here's what it's like to have a Scorpio as your friend.

- **Loyalty**; Scorpios are loyal friends. Once they commit to a friendship they stand by it for the long run. Trust is of great importance to them. As such they will go above and beyond to protect their friends.
- **Intensity and Passion;** Scorpio friends are renowned for their intensity and passion. They approach their friendships with fervent energy and invest deeply. They aim to ensure that their friends feel loved and supported.
- **Depth**; Scorpios dive into the depths of emotions encouraging their friends to do the same. They are the kind of companions with whom you can share feelings without fear of judgment or criticism.
- **Honesty**; Honesty holds important value for Scorpios. Both in themselves and in those they befriend. They will always be honest with you even if the truth is hard to hear. Although they can sometimes come across as blunt. Rest assured that they genuinely care about you.
- **Protective**; Scorpios are incredibly loyal and protective of their friends. They will go to great lengths to support and defend you. Their strong sense of camaraderie ensures they stand by friends during tough times.

- **Empathy and Intuition;** Scorpios possess strong intuition. They are often able to discern their friends' emotions and needs even before they are expressed. Such deep empathy enables them to be there when friends require support.
- **Mystery and Intrigue;** Scorpio friends exude an aura of mystery that's both intriguing and captivating. They willingly discuss topics that others may shy away from. This intellectual stimulation makes their friendships compelling and thought provoking.
- **Challenges;** While Scorpios make great friends it's important to acknowledge that there may be challenges. Dealing with their intensity or occasional possessiveness can prove challenging. In some instances they might hold onto grudges longer than individuals belonging to zodiac signs. In the end their determination to resolve problems and dedication to friendship usually comes out on top.

To sum it up, having a Scorpio as a friend means having a devoted, intense and emotionally profound companion. They bring excitement and intrigue to your life. They are consistently supportive during life's highs and lows. If you appreciate honesty, loyalty and emotional depth, a Scorpio friend in your life is truly valuable.

FAMILY

Family holds great importance for Scorpios. They bring an intense nature into the dynamics of their family life. Overall they approach their family roles with a strong sense of loyalty, protection and emotional depth. Let's take a close look at how Scorpios contribute to the dynamics within their families.

- **Committed**; Scorpios are incredibly loyal to their family. They remain committed to supporting and protecting their loved ones through thick and thin. During challenging times they are often the ones who can be relied upon.
- **Emotional Depth**; Scorpios infuse family relationships with emotional depth. They are often the family members who encourage open and honest communication. As such they create an environment where everyone feels free to express their emotions.
- **Protective**; Scorpios have a protective instinct when it comes to their family. They will go above and beyond to ensure the well being and safety of their loved ones.
- **Empathy and Intuition;** Scorpios possess a strong sense of empathy and intuition. One that allows them to be attuned to the needs of their family. They often have a sense of when something's wrong and are quick to offer support and comfort.
- **Strong Family Bonds**; Scorpios have an ability to form unbreakable bonds within their families. These bonds are built on trust, loyalty and shared experiences. Scorpio family members often confide in each other and provide strength to one another.

- **Resilience and Determination;** Scorpios are renowned for their resilience and determination. As parents or elders, they pass on these qualities, teaching youngsters the importance of perseverance and facing life's challenges head on.
- **Power Struggles;** There can be instances where Scorpios engage in power struggles within the family. Their strong will and desire for control may lead to conflicts with dominant family members. It's important for Scorpios to learn when it is necessary to compromise or let go.
- **Healing and Transformation;** Scorpios possess a transformative quality. They often playing a role in helping their family members grow emotionally and heal from experiences. During times of crisis or personal growth they offer support and guidance.
- **Independence;** Scorpios highly value their independence. This can sometimes cause conflicts within the family during adolescence or early adulthood. They may assert their need for autonomy, challenging controlling family members' acceptance.

In summary Scorpio's contribution to family dynamics is characterized by their loyalty, emotions and a strong protective instinct. They form deep connections and often serve as the emotional pillars within their families. While their intense nature may occasionally lead to conflicts, their unwavering commitment to their loved ones make them invaluable members of any family.

CHALLENGES IN FRIENDSHIPS AND FAMILY RELATIONS

Scorpios are well known for their loyalty, intense emotions and strong connections with others. However they do face challenges when it comes to their friendships and family relationships due to their personality traits. Here are some of the difficulties Scorpios may encounter in these connections.

- **Intensity and Jealousy**; Scorpio's intense passion can sometimes be overwhelming for those to them. Their occasional jealousy and possessiveness may lead to conflicts especially when they feel threatened or insecure in their relationships.
- **Stubbornness**; Scorpio's determination and stubbornness can be both a strength and a hindrance. While it helps them stay focused in situations it may also make it hard for them to compromise.
- **Secretive**; Scorpios tend to be individuals who cherish secrecy. While this adds an element of mystery around them it can also create trust issues. Others might feel left out or uncertain about what Scorpio feels or intends.
- **Depth**; Scorpios possess emotional depth. This is a quality that can both empower and challenge them in relationships. As such they might find it difficult to navigate through emotions at times. They might expect others to match their level of emotional intensity, which could prove unrealistic for some people.

- **Unforgiving**; It can be challenging for Scorpios to forgive easily. They tend to hold onto grudges and struggle to let go of grievances. This can lead to standing conflicts and strained relationships.
- **Controlling**; Scorpios often have a desire for control. This desire for dominance can create tension and conflicts.
- **Closed off;** Scorpios tend to fear vulnerability. They may find it difficult to open up about their emotions and insecurities. Overall it can hinder emotional connections and prevent them from fully expressing themselves.
- **High expectations**; Scorpios have high expectations for their relationships. They place a burden on their friends and family expecting unwavering loyalty. When these expectations are not met they may feel disappointed or hurt.
- **Emotional intensity**; Scorpios emotional intensity can be overwhelming for some people. Friends and family members may occasionally need breaks from the rollercoaster that comes with being in a relationship with a Scorpio.

Despite these challenges it's important to acknowledge that Scorpios bring excellent qualities to their friendships and families. By acknowledging and addressing their challenges Scorpios can cultivate relationships with their loved ones that're more balanced and satisfying. Effective communication, empathy and self awareness serve as tools in overcoming these challenges. Overall working on these challenges can lead to fostering connections that're healthier and more fulfilling.

Throughout this chapter we have embarked on an exploration of Scorpio individuals within the context of their friendships and family dynamics. With their loyalty, passion and intricate emotional nature Scorpios establish connections that are both captivating and transformative. As we wrap up this chapter lets take a moment to think about the Scorpio people in our lives. They are the friends who always have our backs and the family members who support us no matter what. Let's embrace their intensity, value their loyalty and approach the challenges that come with Scorpio connections, with empathy and understanding. These relationships are intricate and meaningful showcasing how Scorpios influence can truly transform the lives of those they care about.

CHAPTER 4:
CAREER AND MONEY

In this chapter we delve into the realm of Scorpio individuals and their connections to their careers and finances. Within this chapter we explore how Scorpios approach their careers with determination, resourcefulness and a yearning for depth. We investigate their leadership qualities, financial expertise and ability to thrive under pressure. From entrepreneurship to healing professions Scorpios exhibit a range of career preferences. Additionally this chapter addresses the obstacles that Scorpios may encounter in their careers and offers strategies to overcome them. By doing so we aim to assist Scorpio individuals in leveraging their strengths while navigating challenges.

Join us as we uncover the secrets behind Scorpios success in the world of work and finance. Whether you are a Scorpio seeking guidance on your career journey or simply intrigued by the approach that Scorpios take towards wealth and work this chapter serves as an invaluable resource.

CAREER ASPIRATIONS

Scorpios approach their career aspirations with the level of intensity and passion that they bring to other aspects of their lives. They are recognized for their determination, resourcefulness and ability to excel in a range of fields. Let's take a look at the career preferences and professional aspirations commonly associated with Scorpios.

- **Craving for Depth**; Scorpios thrive in careers that allow them to dive deep into their work. They are naturally drawn to professions where they can uncover truths, solve problems and explore the underlying motivations behind people or systems. This makes them well suited for careers in fields such as psychology, criminology, research and investigative journalism.
- **Leadership Skills;** Scorpios possess leadership qualities. They have a knack for taking charge and propelling projects forward. Due to this talent they often find themselves attracted to positions of authority. For example in management roles where they can effectively lead and influence others.
- **Financial Acumen**; Many Scorpios have an interest in finance. They possess sharp money

management skills. As such they tend to excel in careers related to investments, banking services, financial analysis or accounting. Their natural shrewdness combined with their shrewd attitude equips them well for navigating the complexities of the financial world.

- **Entrepreneurial Drive**; The independent spirit and ambition inherent within Scorpios often lead them down the path of entrepreneurship. They are willing to take calculated risks and work tirelessly to transform their ideas into profitable ventures. Their passion and determination drive them to overcome obstacles and achieve their goals.

- **Healing Professions**; Scorpios naturally possess empathy and are drawn towards professions that involve assisting others. They may choose careers in medicine, psychology, counseling or therapy.

Here they can make an impact on people's lives through healing and personal growth.
- **Creative Fields**; Scorpios often have a creative spirit that they express through careers in the arts, music, writing or acting. They approach their pursuits with a sense of passion and emotion creating work that deeply resonates with others.
- **Scientific Research**; Scorpios possess an analytical nature. This makes them well suited for research and exploration. Fields such as biology, chemistry, astronomy and forensics might captivate their interest. Overall they enjoy unraveling the mysteries of the universe.
- **Tech and IT;** With their problem solving skills, Scorpios can excel in the technology and information technology (IT) sectors. They are drawn towards careers, in software development, cybersecurity, data analysis and other tech related domains.
- **Occult and Metaphysical Interests**; Some Scorpios find themselves intrigued by occultism or metaphysical subjects. Careers such as astrology, tarot card reading, spiritual counseling or metaphysical healing.

To summarize Scorpios approach their careers with a sense of purpose, passion and determination. They thrive in roles that allow them to delve into their chosen field, showcase their leadership skills and have an impact on others. Whether they pursue professions, start ventures or engage in creative pursuits. Scorpio's unwavering commitment to excellence and drive for success make them highly accomplished professionals.

CAREER STRENGTHS

Scorpio individuals have a set of unique strengths that often contribute to their success in the workplace. Their intense determination and innate abilities make them highly valued assets in various settings. Let's explore some of the strengths that make Scorpio individuals excel in their careers.

- **Determination and Perseverance**; Scorpios are known for their resolve and persistence. Once they set their sights on a goal or project they pursue it relentlessly. This determination enables them to overcome obstacles and stay focused on achieving their objectives. In conclusion it makes them exceptionally effective in their roles.
- **Resourcefulness**; Scorpios possess a talent for finding solutions to problems. They can think outside the box, which proves invaluable in the workplace. They also excel at discovering unique approaches to tackle challenges and enhance processes.
- **Intuition**; Scorpios have a strong sense of intuition, which allows them to make great decisions. They often trust their gut instincts enabling them to make tough choices in situations such as negotiations, problem solving or decision making.
- **Strong Leadership Skills**; Scorpios inherently possess leadership qualities. They exude confidence, assertiveness and fearlessness when it comes to taking charge when necessary.

- **Emotional Intelligence**; Scorpio individuals possess an understanding of emotions both their own and those of others. This emotional intelligence aids them in building relationships, resolving conflicts and navigating interpersonal dynamics.
- **Attention to Detail**; Scorpios pay attention to the smallest details. They are thorough in their work and often catch errors that others might overlook. This meticulousness ensures that their projects and tasks are executed with precision.
- **Passion and Commitment;** Scorpios bring a passion to their work. They are also fully committed to their responsibilities.
- **Ability to Thrive Under Pressure**; Scorpios excel under pressure. They are known for remaining calm and composed in high stress situations. This resilience enables them to perform well when faced with deadlines or challenging circumstances.
- **Problem Solving Skills**; Scorpios possess an aptitude for problem solving. They enjoy tackling issues and finding solutions. Their analytical mindset coupled with unwavering determination makes them highly adept at resolving challenges.
- **Strategic Thinking Abilities;** Scorpios exhibit strategic thinking skills. They anticipate trends and make decisions that align with long term objectives. This makes them valuable assets, in strategic planning and decision making positions.
- **Dedication to Achieving Excellence**; Scorpios exhibit a dedication to achieving excellence. They set high standards for themselves and take pride in

producing quality work. This commitment often leads to recognition and career growth.

To summarize Scorpio individuals thrive in the workplace due to their perseverance, emotional intelligence and exceptional leadership qualities. Their ability to handle pressure, attention to detail and unwavering commitment, to achieving excellence make them valued team members and leaders.

CHALLENGES IN THE WORKPLACE

Scorpio individuals, while possessing many strengths, also face certain challenges that can impact their professional growth. Recognizing these challenges and implementing strategies to overcome them is crucial for Scorpios to thrive in the workplace. Here are some common challenges faced by Scorpio individuals in their careers and strategies to address them.

INTENSITY AND EMOTIONAL EXPRESSION

- Challenge: Scorpios' intense emotions can sometimes be overwhelming in professional settings. Their passion can come across as intimidating or overly dramatic.
- Strategy: Scorpios can work on managing their emotional intensity by practicing mindfulness. Take deep breaths before responding. Find emotional relief through exercise or creative pursuits.

TENDENCY TO HOLD GRUDGES

- Challenge: Scorpios may have difficulty letting go of past conflicts or grievances. This can hinder collaboration and team dynamics.
- Strategy: Scorpios can benefit from practicing forgiveness. Addressing conflicts directly and seeking resolution is also essential.

DESIRE FOR CONTROL

- Challenge: Scorpios' strong desire for control can lead to micromanagement or reluctance to delegate tasks. This can impede team efficiency and collaboration.
- Strategy: Scorpios can develop trust in their colleagues' abilities and focus on delegating tasks according to their team members' strengths. Learning to let go of control and empowering others can lead to more productive teamwork.

RESISTANCE TO CHANGE

- Challenge: Scorpios may be resistant to change, preferring stability and familiarity in their work environment.
- Strategy: Scorpios can cultivate adaptability by embracing change as an opportunity for growth and learning. They can seek out new challenges and view change as a chance to excel rather than as a threat.

TENDENCY TOWARD SECRECY

- Challenge: Scorpios' secretive nature can lead to a lack of transparency in their professional relationships, potentially eroding trust.
- Strategy: Scorpios can practice open communication and transparency with colleagues and superiors. Sharing information and being open about their intentions can foster trust and strengthen workplace relationships.

DIFFICULTY IN ACCEPTING CONSTRUCTIVE CRITICISM

- Challenge: Scorpios may struggle with receiving constructive criticism, interpreting it as a personal attack rather than an opportunity for improvement.
- Strategy: Scorpios can work on developing a growth mindset, understanding that feedback is essential for development. They can learn to separate their self-worth from criticism and focus on using feedback to enhance their skills.

OVERWHELM FROM HIGH EXPECTATIONS

- Challenge: Scorpios' high expectations for themselves and others can lead to feelings of overwhelm and burnout.
- Strategy: Scorpios can set realistic goals and prioritize self-care. Learning to balance their drive for excellence with self-compassion and

acknowledging their limits is essential for long-term success.

In summary individuals born under the Scorpio zodiac sign can overcome these obstacles by developing self awareness, practicing adaptability and improving their communication and conflict resolution skills. By acknowledging their tendencies and implementing these strategies Scorpios can navigate their lives effectively and continue to thrive in their chosen fields.

Throughout this chapter we have explored the world of Scorpio individuals and their unique approach to careers and finances. The unwavering determination, resourcefulness and intense passion that drive Scorpios serve as guiding principles on their journey towards success in the workplace and financial mastery.

Their innate leadership qualities, ability to handle pressure with grace and relentless pursuit of excellence distinguish them in any setting. However we have also examined the challenges that may arise for Scorpios such, as intensity and resistance to change. By acknowledging these challenges head on and implementing strategies to overcome them Scorpios can fully unleash their potential within the realm.

As we bring this chapter to a close we encourage you to embrace the Scorpio approach when shaping your career path and financial journey. If you happen to be a Scorpio looking to enhance your abilities or if you are simply fascinated by their characteristics. Allow yourself to be inspired by the drive, persistence and strength that Scorpio individuals exhibit. By staying committed and employing strategic thought processes Scorpios can emerge as successful architects of their financial futures.

CHAPTER 5: SELF-IMPROVEMENT

In this chapter we will dive into the journey of self discovery for Scorpios. We will explore how they harness their strengths, confront their weaknesses head on and navigate the path towards self improvement. Come along with us as we uncover the secrets behind Scorpios unwavering dedication to growth. We will also provide strategies and insights that can inspire anyone. Regardless of whether they're a Scorpio or not. So whether you are a Scorpio seeking excellence or someone intrigued by the approach that Scorpios take in bettering themselves this chapter will serve as your guide.

PERSONAL GROWTH AND SELF DEVELOPMENT

Personal growth and self development hold significance for individuals born under the zodiac sign of Scorpio. Here are some essential elements pertaining to growth and development specific to Scorpio individuals.

- **Embracing Vulnerability;** Scorpios are renowned for their depth and intensity. A significant aspect of growth for a Scorpio involves embracing vulnerability allowing oneself to express emotions openly. This process fosters connections with others. Ultimately it cultivates a deeper understanding of oneself.

- **Self Reflection**; Self reflection is highly beneficial for Scorpios. Their introspective nature empowers them to delve into their psyche exploring their motivations, desires and fears in detail. Activities such as journaling, meditation or therapy serve as tools for Scorpios to gain insights into their worlds.
- **Life Altering Experiences**; Scorpios often seek experiences that push them beyond their comfort zones. These experiences can take the form of challenges, travel adventures or even spiritual journeys.
- **Embracing Change;** Due to their desire for control Scorpios tend to be resistant, towards change. However personal growth requires embracing change as a part of life's progression. Scorpios can enhance their adaptability by embracing change by seeing it as an opportunity for growth rather than a threat.
- **Letting go**; This is essential for Scorpios to grow personally as they have a tendency to hold onto grudges and past hurts. By practicing forgiveness and releasing resentments they can embark on a journey of healing and liberation. It's important for Scorpios to find a balance between control and surrender since they may sometimes become controlling both with themselves and their surroundings. By trusting the process and letting go of tension they can develop personally.
- **Compassion**; The innate empathy of Scorpios allows them to deeply connect with others emotions. As part of their growth they can refine their abilities and use them to foster understanding and compassion in their relationships.

- **Confidence**; Scorpios often second guess themselves due to their personality tendencies. Personal growth involves building self trust, embracing instincts and making confident decisions.
- **Seek help**; Seeking guidance from mentors, therapists or spiritual advisors can be beneficial for Scorpios on their growth journey as these individuals provide insights and support. Many Scorpios are naturally drawn to metaphysical topics which offer an avenue for purposeful exploration and connection with the universe
- **Constant learning**; Scorpios are naturally curious with a desire for knowledge. They believe that personal growth is achieved through learning and self improvement. Scorpios can satisfy their curiosity by exploring interests and acquiring new skills.

To sum up personal growth and development for Scorpio individuals involve embracing vulnerability reflecting on oneself engaging in experiences and being open to change. As they navigate these aspects of growth Scorpios can unlock their potential, build deeper connections with others and embark on a journey of self discovery and transformation that leads to a more fulfilling and meaningful life.

HARNESSING SCORPIO STRENGTHS AND OVERCOMING WEAKNESSES

Harnessing the strengths of Scorpio and overcoming their weaknesses is a life changing journey that involves self awareness, personal growth and a commitment to embracing their qualities. Here's how they can effectively utilize their strengths while addressing any areas for improvement.

UTILIZING STRENGTHS

- **Determination**; Scorpios are determined individuals. To harness this strength they can set concrete goals. Break them down into achievable steps. Their unwavering determination will drive them to accomplish the ambitious objectives.
- **Emotional Depth**; Scorpios profound emotional depth can be an asset in relationships and creativity. They can leverage this strength to establish connections with others and channel their emotions into empathetic endeavors.
- **Leadership Qualities**; Scorpios naturally possess leadership abilities that can propel them into roles.

To make the most of this strength they should actively seek out leadership positions where their assertiveness and passion can inspire and motivate others.

- **Resourcefulness**; The resourcefulness of Scorpios is invaluable when it comes to problem solving. They should apply this strength to find solutions in their personal lives.
- **Empathy**; The empathetic nature of Scorpios enables them to deeply understand others.They can utilize this strength to foster connections, resolve disagreements and provide support for those who require it.

OVERCOMING WEAKNESSES

- **Jealousy**; Scorpios have the ability to address their emotions and feelings of jealousy by practicing techniques like mindfulness, meditation and open communication with their loved ones. These strategies can assist them in managing these emotions
- **Stubbornness**; It is beneficial for Scorpios to cultivate flexibility and adaptability. They can achieve this by learning to compromise and considering perspectives in both professional settings.
- **Secrecy**; Scorpios can enhance transparency within their relationships by opening up and sharing their thoughts and emotions with trusted individuals. Building trust takes time. It can result in connections.

- **Resistance to Change**; To overcome their resistance towards change Scorpios can gradually expose themselves to experiences. They can start with changes before moving on to significant transitions.
- **Difficulty Accepting Criticism**; Scorpios should view criticism as an opportunity for growth than a personal attack. Reminding themselves that feedback helps them improve and evolve will aid in accepting criticism
- **Excessive Expectations**; Managing expectations is important, for Scorpios. Setting goals that're attainable is crucial; it is essential for them to understand that perfection is not always achievable. Celebrating successes along the way is equally important.

SEEKING SUPPORT

Scorpios can benefit from seeking support in their journey of harnessing strengths and overcoming weaknesses. This support can come from various sources, including:

- **Therapy**: Professional counseling or therapy can help Scorpios address deep-seated emotional issues and develop healthier coping mechanisms.
- **Mentorship**: Seeking guidance from mentors or role models who have successfully navigated similar challenges can be highly beneficial.
- **Peer Support**: Sharing experiences and insights with peers who understand their struggles can provide Scorpios with valuable perspectives and encouragement.
- **Self-Help Resources:** Scorpios can explore self-help books, workshops, and online resources that offer practical strategies for personal growth and development.

In conclusion Scorpios possess a set of strengths and weaknesses that shape their lives. By utilizing their strengths, addressing their areas for improvement and seeking support when necessary, Scorpios can embark on a journey of self improvement. Ultimately this will lead to a fulfilling and harmonious life.

Throughout this chapter we have delved deeply into the commitment of Scorpio individuals, towards self improvement. With their determination and emotional depth Scorpios naturally seek self awareness and transformation. As we wrap up this chapter lets take a moment to reflect on the aspects of the Scorpio journey and the positive outlook for their potential.

Scorpio individuals have potential for growth and self improvement. With unwavering determination, depth and innate strengths they are capable of achieving milestones in both their personal and professional lives. As Scorpios continue to embrace their vulnerability, let go of the past and build trust in themselves they will find themselves following a path of self discovery that is constantly evolving. Their strong passion and unwavering determination will drive them forward allowing them to create an impact not, in their own lives but also in the lives of those around them. May the Scorpios journey towards self improvement serve as an inspiration for all of us to embark on our paths of growth and transformation!

CHAPTER 6:
THE YEAR AHEAD

In this chapter we'll be shedding light on the challenges and opportunities that are waiting for Scorprios in the year ahead. As we navigate through the events and planetary influences shaping the year we'll delve into how these cosmic forces impact Scorpios love life, career, finances, health and much more. From enlightening eclipses that reveal truths to empowering transits fueling Scorpios ambitions each astrological event plays a vital role in shaping the path forward.

Join us as we unravel the mysteries of the universe and offer guidance on how Scorpio individuals can maximize opportunities while navigating challenges throughout the year. Whether you're a Scorpio seeking to understand the energies at play or someone captivated by Scorpios journey in the year ahead, this chapter provides an enthralling exploration of celestial forces shaping destinies. So come along on a captivating journey into what the upcoming year has, in store for Scorpio individuals.

SCORPIO HOROSCOPE GUIDE FOR THE YEAR AHEAD

This year Scorpio you can look forward to a journey of growth and self discovery. The universe is aligning to help you unveil truths, make life changes and tap into your inner strength. While there may be obstacles, along the way your determination and enthusiasm will steer you towards success.

CAREER AND FINANCES

Your professional life will experience advancements this year. Exciting opportunities and challenges will arise, providing a chance for you to showcase your leadership abilities. You might find yourself in a position of authority where your skills are highly valued. When it comes to finances, focus on making wise investments and financial diligence.

Scorpio individuals can anticipate a dynamic year in their careers and finances, influenced by celestial events. Here's a glimpse of what to expect:

- **Saturn Transits:** Saturn's presence may bring responsibilities and challenges in your career. Embrace these as opportunities for growth and consider long-term goals.
- **Mars Transits:** Mars will energize Scorpio's career sector. This is an excellent time for taking bold actions, launching projects and asserting your leadership in the workplace.
- **Jupiter Transits:** The influence of Jupiter can expand your financial horizons. Be open to new opportunities, investments, or financial growth during this time.

LOVE AND RELATIONSHIPS

In matters of the heart anticipate a year brimming with emotions and transformative encounters. If you're currently in a relationship it will deepen further and strengthen over time. Single Scorpios may cross paths with someone who deeply resonates with their soul. Be aware of feelings like jealousy or possessiveness that can strain relationships. Open communication and trust are pillars for nurturing connections.

In the realm of love and relationships, Scorpio individuals will find the astrological events of the year bringing both challenges and opportunities. Here's a closer look at how these celestial occurrences may influence Scorpio's love life:

- **Solar and Lunar Eclipses**: Eclipses can shake up Scorpio's relationships by bringing hidden issues to the surface. Pay close attention to the Solar Eclipse and the Lunar Eclipse. These dates may prompt important conversations and decisions about your romantic partnerships.
- **Venus Retrograde:** Venus retrogrades can affect Scorpios emotional landscape. During this period be prepared for relationship reassessments. Past romantic patterns may resurface, allowing you to make necessary changes for more meaningful connections.
- **Jupiter Transits:** Jupiter's positive influence can bring growth and optimism to Scorpio's love life. When Jupiter transits you may experience expanded horizons and the opportunity to meet someone who ignites your passions.

HEALTH AND WELLNESS

Taking care of your emotional well being should take precedence this year. Prioritize stress management techniques along with exercise routines and maintaining a healthy diet. Take part in relaxation techniques such as meditation or yoga to keep your mind and emotions balanced. Prioritize self care to maintain your energy and resilience.

Scorpio individuals should pay close attention to their health and wellness in light of the year's astrological events. Here are some insights:

- **Mercury Retrograde:** During Mercury retrogrades your stress levels may increase. Practice stress management techniques, maintain a balanced diet, and prioritize self-care to ensure emotional and physical well-being.
- **Jupiter Transits:** Jupiter's positive influence can enhance your overall vitality. Use this time to focus on fitness, well-balanced nutrition, and relaxation practices for optimal health.

PERSONAL GROWTH AND SELF-DISCOVERY

The year ahead offers abundant opportunities for personal growth and self-discovery for Scorpio individuals. Here's how to make the most of it:

- **Solar and Lunar Eclipses:** Eclipses, especially the Solar Eclipse encourage Scorpios to dive deep into self-discovery. Embrace introspection and

explore your passions, desires, and hidden potentials.
- **Mars Transits:** Mars' dynamic influence empowers Scorpio to take action. Channel this energy into self-improvement, goals and exploring your passions.
- **Jupiter Transits:** Jupiter's positive energy supports your personal growth journey. Embrace new experiences, engage in spiritual practices and seek wisdom to enhance your self-discovery.

Self Development and Spirituality

This year presents a chance for growth. Embrace introspection and self discovery. Explore your spirituality. Engage in practices that deepen your connection with yourself. Trusting your instincts will provide guidance during times.

Travel and Excitement

Consider embarking on adventures and exploring different places this year. Venturing into new territories will broaden your horizons and offer fresh perspectives. Stay open to spontaneity as some magical moments may arise from unexpected journeys.

Potential Challenges to Be Cautious About

Be mindful of becoming overly controlling or possessive in your relationships as this can lead to conflicts. Your intense nature might also make it challenging for you to embrace change. Remember that growth often requires stepping outside of your comfort zone. It's important to maintain a work life balance to avoid burnout.

Overall the upcoming year holds promise for individuals born under the sign of Scorpio. Embrace the transformative energies, trust your wisdom and remain receptive to both opportunities and challenges that come along the way.

With your resolve and enthusiastic nature you have the ability to turn this year into a satisfying phase, in your life's adventure.

By approaching the happenings with mindfulness and self awareness Scorpio individuals can tap into their potential for professional development, nurture their relationships and prioritize their health and well being in the coming year. Stay tuned for the upcoming year promises a voyage of self discovery, growth and transformation.

KEY ASTROLOGICAL EVENTS

Key astrological events can significantly impact Scorpio individuals. They influence various aspects of their lives, including relationships, career and much more. Here are some notable astrological events and their potential impact on Scorpio individuals:

SOLAR AND LUNAR ECLIPSES

- Impact: Eclipses often bring about significant life changes and transformations. They may prompt Scorpios to reevaluate their goals, make important decisions, or address unresolved issues.

- Advice: Use eclipse periods for self-reflection and setting new intentions. Embrace change and be open to opportunities for personal growth.

MERCURY RETROGRADE

- Impact: Mercury retrogrades can disrupt communication and travel plans. Scorpios may experience misunderstandings or delays in their work and personal relationships.
- Advice: Practice patience and double-check details during retrograde periods. Use this time for introspection and revisiting past projects.

JUPITER TRANSITS

- Impact: When Jupiter transits Scorpio or favorable areas of their chart, it can bring luck, expansion and personal growth. This influence may lead to new opportunities and increased optimism.
- Advice: Embrace Jupiter's positive energy by being open to new experiences, taking calculated risks and pursuing goals.

SATURN TRANSITS

- Impact: Saturn transits can bring challenges and lessons, often in the form of responsibilities or limitations. Scorpios may face obstacles that test their patience and determination.
- Advice: Approach Saturn transits with discipline and resilience. Focus on long-term goals and the

lessons that come with adversity, knowing that they contribute to personal growth.

VENUS RETROGRADE

- Impact: Venus retrogrades can affect Scorpio's romantic and social life. Relationships may undergo reassessment and unresolved issues may resurface.
- Advice: Use this period for introspection in relationships. Reevaluate what truly matters in your connections, and address any unresolved issues with empathy and communication.

MARS TRANSITS

- Impact: Mars transits can boost Scorpio's energy and drive. These periods are excellent for taking action, pursuing goals and initiating new projects.
- Advice: Make the most of Mars' dynamic energy by channeling it into your ambitions and physical activities. Be mindful of not becoming overly aggressive in your pursuits.

NEW MOON AND FULL MOON PHASES

- Impact: New Moon phases are ideal for setting intentions and initiating projects, while Full Moons bring culmination and closure. Scorpios may find these phases emotionally charged.
- Advice: Align your intentions with New Moons and use Full Moons for reflection and release.

Harness lunar energies for personal growth and manifestation.

Through astrologys lens we have uncovered the challenges and opportunities that Scorpios may encounter in their lives. The celestial events, from revealing eclipses that bring truths to empowering transits act as guides on this captivating journey. Individual birth charts, which consider the time and place of birth also play a significant role in how these astrological events impact Scorpio individuals. Additionally, consulting with an astrologer can provide personalized insights into how these events affect specific aspects of their lives. Overall, Scorpios can navigate these astrological events with mindfulness, adaptability and a focus on personal growth.

Dear Scorpio, your unwavering determination, intensity and emotional depth will serve as your allies as you navigate through the currents. Embrace challenges as chances for growth. Seize moments of alignment to propel yourself forward. Trust your instincts wholeheartedly while allowing your passion to guide you like a star. May this chapter be a source of insight and inspiration as you embark on your voyage among the stars. No matter the challenges or ease you encounter in life, always remember that you have the strength to overcome and the ability to thrive.

As individuals born under the zodiac sign Scorpio move forward into the year they understand that both themselves and the universe are constantly evolving. Embrace this journey. Embrace the influence of the stars and embrace your limitless potential. The celestial tapestry above illuminates your destiny eagerly waiting for you to weave a tale of growth, exploration and fulfillment.

CHAPTER 7:
FAMOUS SCORPIO PERSONALITIES

In the tapestry of astrology Scorpio stands out as a sign known for its intensity, determination and irresistible charm. People born under this sign are recognized for their dedication and the ability to make a lasting impact on the world. Within this chapter we embark on a journey through the lives of some famous Scorpio individuals who have made their mark in the realms of art, entertainment, politics and more. These Scorpios have not only shaped their respective fields but have also captured the admiration of people worldwide.

As we delve into their captivating stories we will explore the traits and characteristics that have propelled these individuals to greatness. From the realm of music where Scorpio's intensity shines brightly to the world of art where their deep emotions find expression. These remarkable personalities exemplify the potential that comes with being born under the constellation of Scorpio. Join us on this journey as we celebrate the achievements, legacies and enduring allure of Scorpio personalities. Their stories stand as a testament to the power of passion, resilience and mysterious charm that define this sign.

CIARA

- Date of Birth: October 25, 1985.

- Brief Biography: Ciara is a Grammy Award-winning singer, songwriter and dancer known for her chart-topping hits like "Goodies" and "1, 2 Step." She has had a successful career in the music industry.
- Scorpio Traits: Ciara exhibits Scorpio traits such as intensity, determination and charisma.
- Impact: Ciara's music has made a significant impact in the world of R&B and pop music, earning her numerous awards and a dedicated fan base.
- Personal Life: She is married to NFL quarterback Russell Wilson. Together they are known for their philanthropic efforts.

WILL DURANT

- Date of Birth: November 5, 1885.
- Brief Biography: Will Durant was an American historian and philosopher. He is best known for co-authoring "The Story of Civilization" with his wife, Ariel Durant. Their work on history and philosophy is highly regarded.
- Scorpio Traits: Will Durant exhibited Scorpio traits such as deep thinking, analytical skills and dedication to intellectual pursuits.
- Impact: Durant's work left a lasting legacy, influencing generations of scholars and readers interested in history and philosophy.
- Personal Life: Will Durant had a lifelong intellectual partnership with his wife, Ariel Durant.

Their collaborative efforts are celebrated in the world of literature.

JOE BIDEN

- Date of Birth: November 20, 1942.
- Brief Biography: Joe Biden is the 46th President of the United States. He also served as Vice President under President Barack Obama from 2009 to 2017. His political career spans several decades.

- Scorpio Traits: Joe Biden embodies Scorpio traits like determination, resilience and a strong commitment to public service.
- Impact: His election as President marked a significant moment in U.S. history. Furthermore his long political career has had a substantial impact on American politics.

- Personal Life: Joe Biden has faced personal tragedies, including the loss of his wife and daughter. These have shaped his empathy and leadership style.

CHARLES III (KING CHARLES)

- Date of Birth: November 14, 1948.
- Brief Biography: Charles III, also known as King Charles, is king of the British throne. He has been a prominent figure in the British royal family and has focused on various charitable and environmental causes.
- Scorpio Traits: King Charles exhibits Scorpio traits such as strong leadership qualities and a dedication to social and environmental issues.
- Impact: His role within the British monarchy and his commitment to charitable work have made a lasting impact on the United Kingdom and beyond.
- Personal Life: He has been married to Diana, Princess of Wales, and Camilla, Duchess of Cornwall. He is a father to Prince William and Prince Harry.

JULIA ROBERTS

- Date of Birth: October 28, 1967.
- Brief Biography: Julia Roberts is an Academy Award-winning actress. She is known for her iconic roles in films such as "Pretty Woman," "Erin Brockovich," and "My Best Friend's Wedding."

- Scorpio Traits: Julia Roberts possesses Scorpio traits like charisma, intensity and emotional expressiveness.
- Impact: She has had a profound influence on Hollywood. She remains one of the most beloved actresses of her generation.
- Personal Life: Julia Roberts has been in the spotlight for her relationships and family life.

TONYA HARDING

- Date of Birth: November 12, 1970.
- Brief Biography: Tonya Harding is a former professional figure skater. She gained notoriety for her involvement in the attack on fellow skater Nancy Kerrigan. Her career was marked by both success and controversy.
- Scorpio Traits: Tonya Harding displayed Scorpio traits such as competitiveness, determination and intensity.
- Impact: Her career and her role in the Kerrigan incident garnered significant media attention and controversy.
- Personal Life: She has faced legal issues and challenges in her personal life.

BILL GATES

- Date of Birth: October 28, 1955.
- Brief Biography: Bill Gates is a co-founder of Microsoft Corporation. He is one of the world's wealthiest individuals. He is also a prominent

philanthropist and has had a significant impact on the technology industry.
- Scorpio Traits: Bill Gates exemplifies Scorpio traits such as determination, strategic thinking and a focus on innovation.
- Impact: His contributions to the technology sector and his philanthropic work through the Bill and Melinda Gates Foundation.
- Personal Life: Bill Gates is known for his philanthropic efforts. He was married to Melinda Gates for many years before their divorce.

DRAKE

- Date of Birth: October 24, 1986.
- Brief Biography: Drake is a Canadian rapper, singer and actor known for his chart-topping music career. He has won multiple Grammy

Awards and is one of the most influential artists in hip-hop.
- Scorpio Traits: Drake embodies Scorpio traits such as emotional depth, charisma and creativity.
- Impact: His music has had a significant impact on the hip-hop and R&B genres. He has a massive global fan base.
- Personal Life: Drake is known for keeping his personal life relatively private. He has been involved in various philanthropic endeavors.

GRACE KELLY

- Date of Birth: November 12, 1929.
- Brief Biography: Grace Kelly was an American actress who later became Princess Grace of Monaco after marrying Prince Rainier III. She was known for her elegance and acting talent.
- Scorpio Traits: Grace Kelly exhibited Scorpio traits such as grace, allure and emotional depth.
- Impact: Her career in Hollywood and her role as Princess Grace of Monaco made her an iconic figure known for her beauty and philanthropic efforts.
- Personal Life: She married Prince Rainier III of Monaco. She became known for her humanitarian work and dedication to the principality.

KATY PERRY

- Date of Birth: October 25, 1984.

- Brief Biography: Katy Perry is a multi-platinum-selling singer, songwriter and television judge. She is also well known for hits like "Firework" and "Roar."
- Scorpio Traits: Katy Perry exhibits Scorpio traits such as intensity, creativity and a magnetic stage presence.
- Impact: Her music has had a significant influence in the pop music industry. She is celebrated for her empowering anthems and unique style.
- Personal Life: Katy Perry has been involved in various charitable causes.

PABLO PICASSO

- Date of Birth: October 25, 1881.
- Brief Biography: Pablo Picasso was one of the most influential artists of the 20th century. He was known for pioneering the Cubist movement and creating iconic works such as "Guernica."
- Scorpio Traits: Picasso embodied Scorpio traits such as intense creativity, a profound sense of emotion. He had a penchant for pushing artistic boundaries.
- Impact: His contributions to art redefined the possibilities of visual expression and continue to inspire artists worldwide.
- Personal Life: Picasso's personal life was as dynamic as his art. He had multiple relationships and a complex family history.

GEORGIA O'KEEFFE

- Date of Birth: November 15, 1887.
- Brief Biography: Georgia O'Keeffe was an American modernist artist. She was known for her iconic paintings of flowers, landscapes and abstract forms.
- Scorpio Traits: O'Keeffe exhibited Scorpio traits such as passion, a deep connection to nature and a unique perspective on art.
- Impact: Her pioneering work in American modernism. Her contribution to the art world continues to be celebrated and studied.
- Personal Life: She was known for her close relationship with photographer Alfred Stieglitz and her solitary life in New Mexico.

These remarkable individuals who were born under the Scorpio zodiac sign have made a lasting impact on art, entertainment, technology and more. Their unique talents and personalities reflect the depth and complexity often associated with Scorpio individuals.

As our exploration of Scorpio personalities comes to a close we are left with an admiration for the intricate nature that characterizes this mysterious astrological sign. From the realms of entertainment, art, politics and beyond these Scorpio individuals have displayed unwavering determination, intensity and passion. What brings together these renowned Scorpio personalities is their ability to transcend boundaries, challenge conventions and leave a mark in their fields. As we honor their achievements and legacies we also celebrate the potential that lies within each individual born under the sign of Scorpio. Their stories stand as proof of the strength of passion, resilience and the mysterious allure that characterizes this zodiac sign.

As we conclude this chapter let us draw inspiration from the lasting impact Scorpio individuals have left behind. Let them remind us that embracing our emotions and pursuing our desires can guide us towards remarkable achievements.

CONCLUSION

As we near the end of our exploration into the Scorpio zodiac sign we arrive at this conclusion. Here we bring together the range of information we've acquired to shed light on the true essence of Scorpio. Now let us present a comprehensive understanding of this mysterious astrological sign. Firstly we will summarize the key points from the chapters.

- **Chapter 1 History and Mythology;** In this chapter, we delved into the historical and mythological roots of Scorpio. We discovered how ancient civilizations, from Babylon to Greece, revered the scorpion as a symbol of transformation and regeneration. The myth of Scorpio's association with Orion and the scorpion's sting as a means of protection provided insights into Scorpio's protective and transformative nature.
- **Chapter 2 Love and Compatibility;** In this chapter we explored Scorpio's approach to love and compatibility. We saw their intense and passionate nature influence romance. Understanding Scorpio's love traits, preferences and compatibility can lead to more fulfilling relationships. In turn we saw how Scorpios are most compatible with water signs like Cancer and Pisces. Together they often share profound emotional connections.

- **Chapter 3 Friends and Family;** In the realm of friendships and family dynamics, we uncovered how Scorpios value loyalty, trust and emotional depth. Their protective nature extends to their loved ones. Overall it makes them fiercely loyal and supportive. Both as a friend and in the family dynamic. We also explored the challenges Scorpios may encounter in these relationships.
- **Chapter 4 Finance and Career;** In this chapter we explored Scorpio's career preferences and strengths. Notable was their determination, focus and ambition in the workplace. They thrive in roles that require research, problem-solving and transformation. We also discussed the challenges they might face and strategies to overcome them, along with their financial attitudes and aspirations.
- **Chapter 5 - Self-Improvement;** This chapter delved into personal growth and development for Scorpios. We discussed harnessing their strengths, overcoming weaknesses and provided guidance on self-improvement. Scorpios were encouraged to embrace introspection, set goals and pursue their passions for transformative growth.
- **Chapter 6 - Scorpio in the Year Ahead:** In this chapter, we explored how astrological events would influence Scorpio individuals' lives in areas. Special attention was given to significant dates and time periods that hold particular significance for Scorpios throughout the year.
- **Chapter 7 - Famous Scorpio Personalities:** In this chapter we celebrated the achievements and legacies of famous Scorpio personalities from various fields. These individuals, including artists,

leaders, and innovators, showcased the intensity, determination, and magnetic allure that define Scorpios. Their stories serve as inspiration for all Scorpio individuals to harness their unique qualities for greatness.

As we wrap up our exploration of the essence of Scorpio, take a moment to reflect on the facets of this passionate and transformative zodiac sign. Whether you identify as a Scorpio on a journey of self discovery or simply find yourself intrigued by the spirit of Scorpio. The knowledge shared in this book may empower you to embrace your emotions, harness your determination and appreciate the allure that comes with being a Scorpio.

Throughout this book our focus has been, on shedding light on the nature of Scorpio celebrating its intensity, unwavering determination and irresistible charm. We have delved into historical accounts, mythology and practical insights to provide you with an understanding of what it means to be a Scorpio. Our aim is to offer guidance and inspiration not for individuals who identify as Scorpios but for those fascinated by their distinctive qualities.

Ultimately our main goal is for readers to grasp that being a Scorpio is an empowering experience. By embracing their intensity, determination and magnetic allure individuals born under this sign can embark on a path of personal growth and achieve extraordinary feats.

In conclusion astrology provides us with a lens through which we can gain insights into ourselves as well as others. The zodiac sign of Scorpio serves as a reminder that embracing change and personal growth is crucial in life. Those who possess the qualities of Scorpios have the opportunity to unlock their potential making a lasting impact on the world.

To all Scorpios out we encourage you to display your intensity, draw strength from your determination and share your magnetic charm as a precious gift. Your presence enriches our world and your journey, as a Scorpio is a tapestry woven with threads of passion, resilience and limitless possibilities.

As we conclude this exploration of Scorpio may you continue to shine as beings. Embrace your strengths and let them empower you as you leave your mark on the universe with each step you take on your journey.

www.ingramcontent.com/pod-product-compliance
Lightning Source LLC
Chambersburg PA
CBHW050444010526
44118CB00013B/1679